Animal

COLORING BOOKS

FOR TEENS

COLOR TEST PAGE

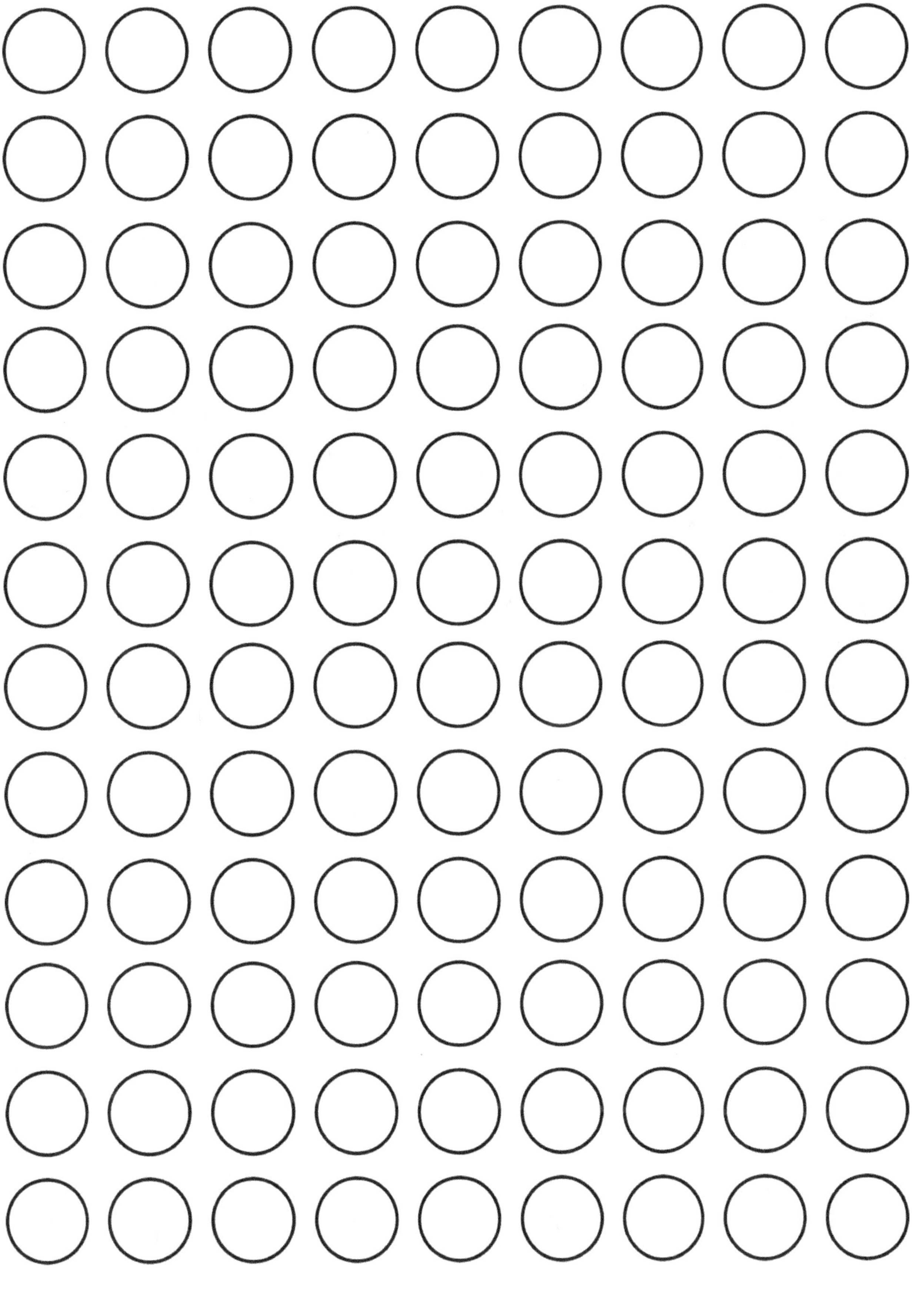

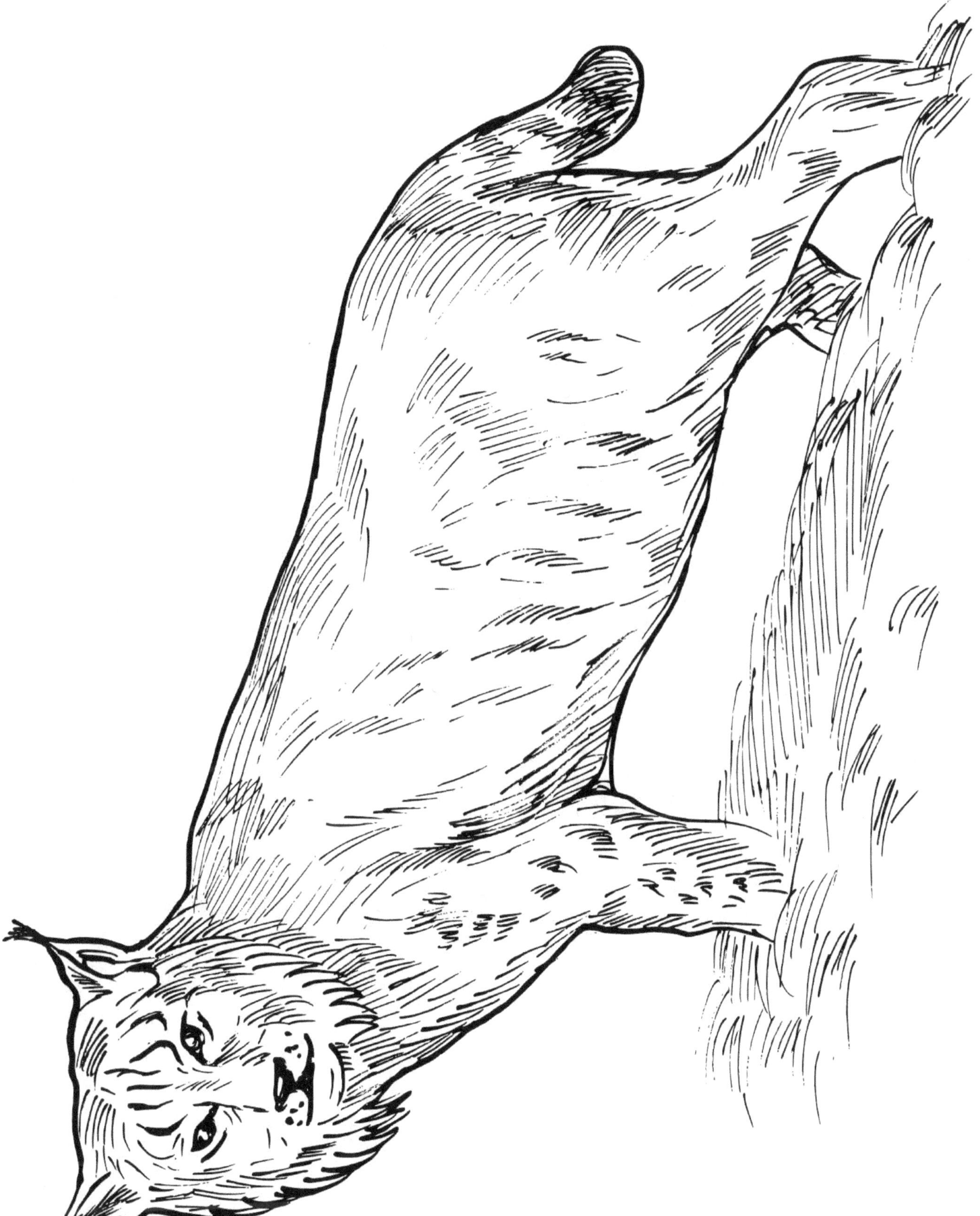

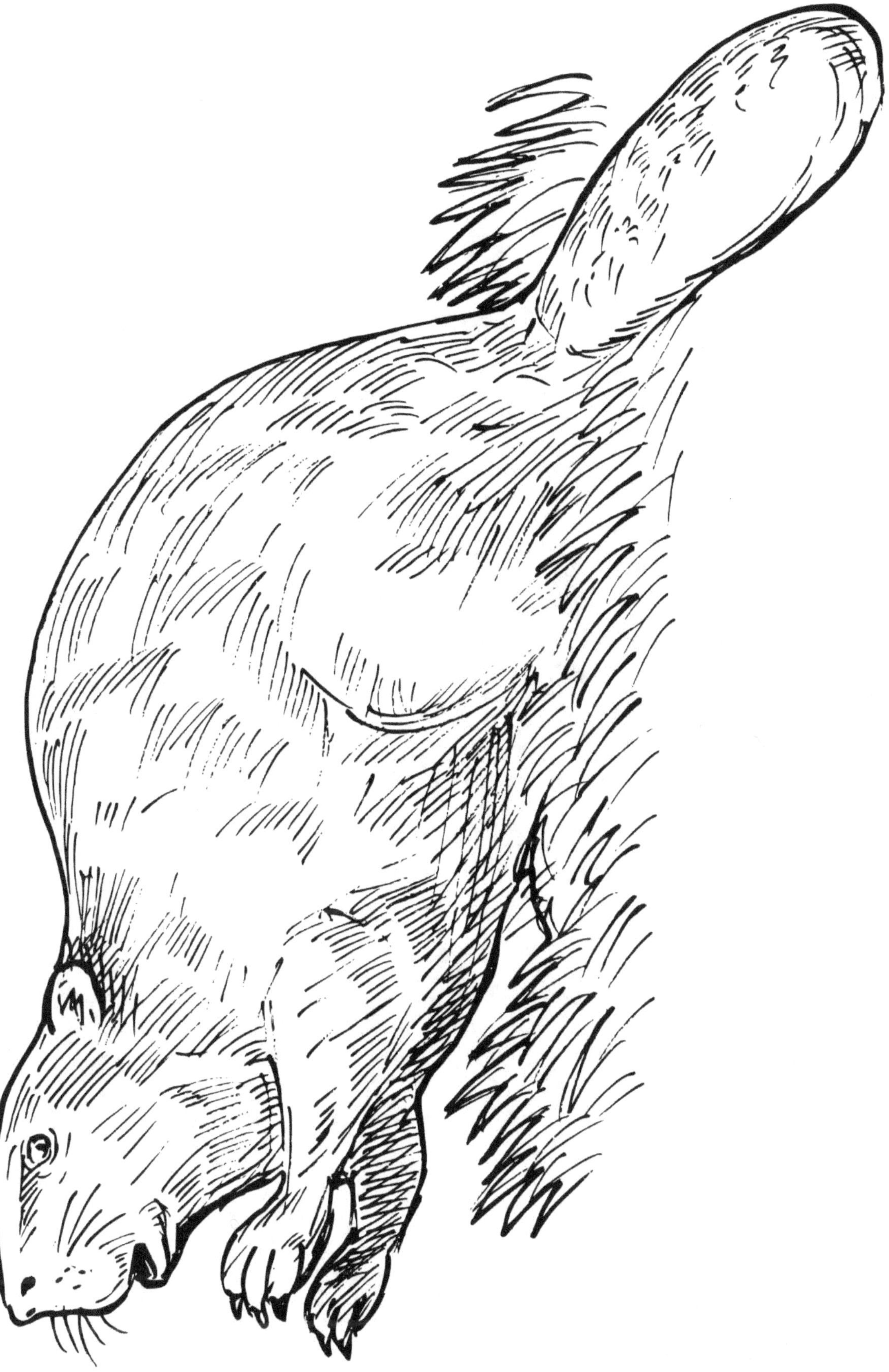

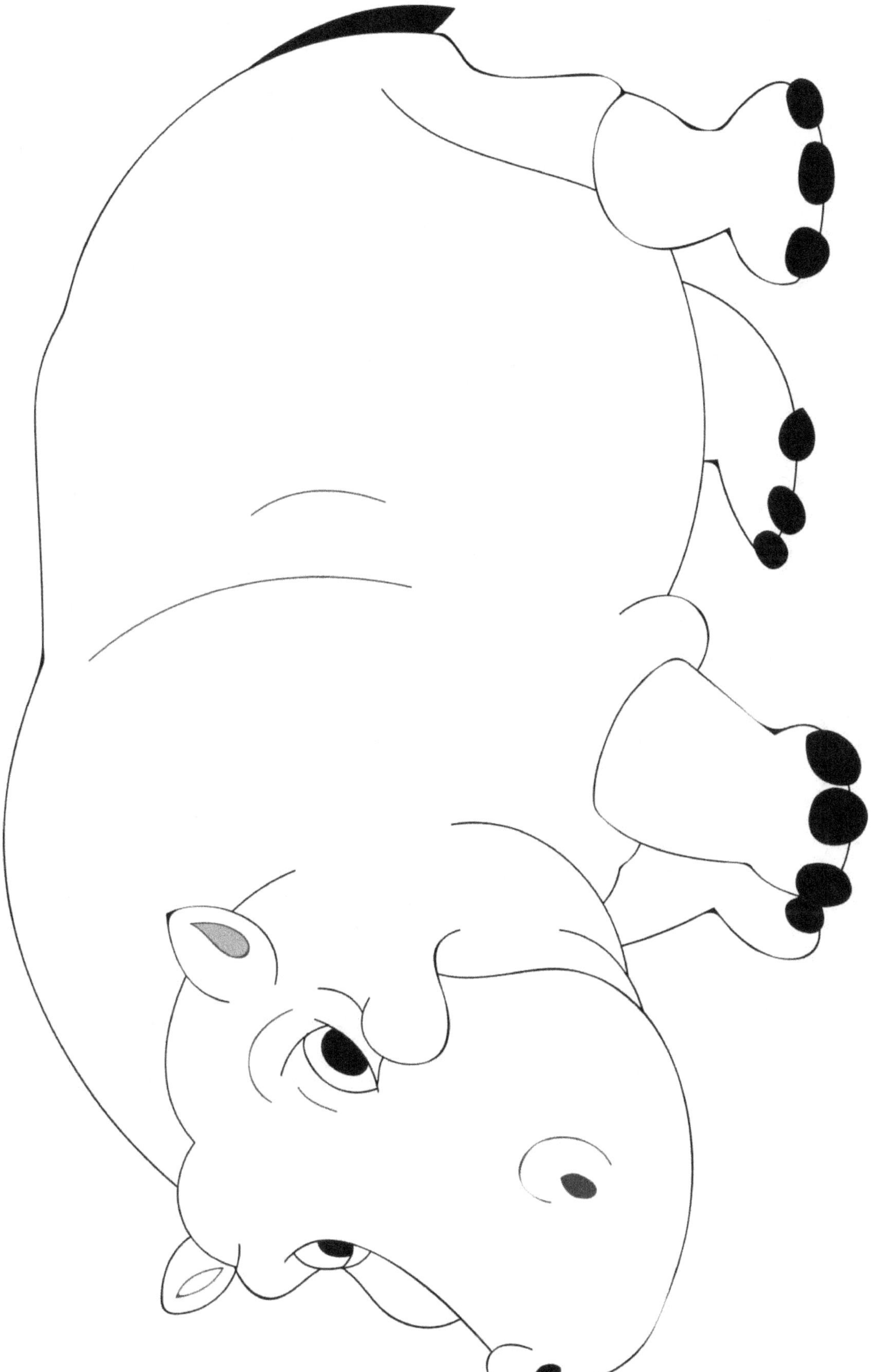

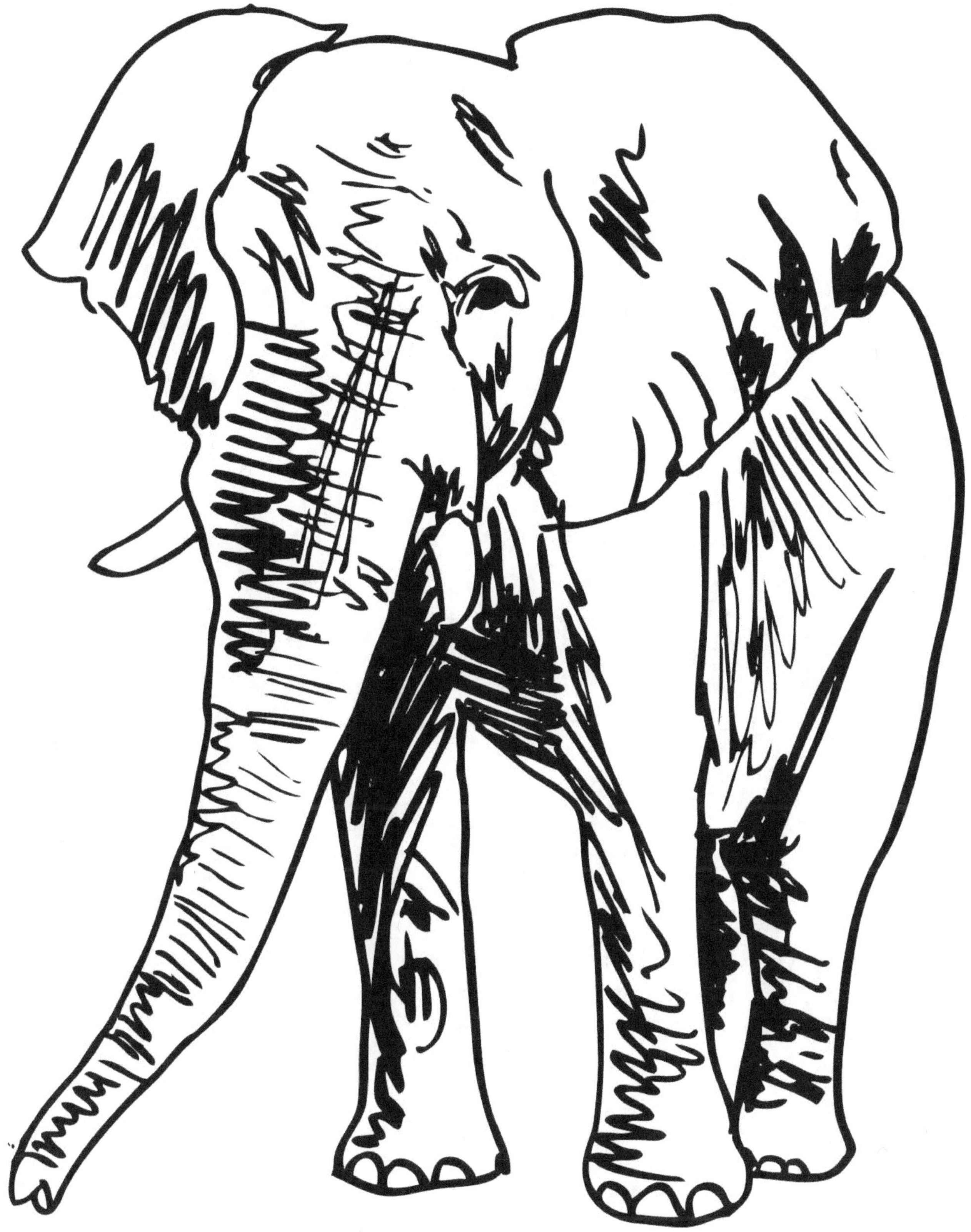

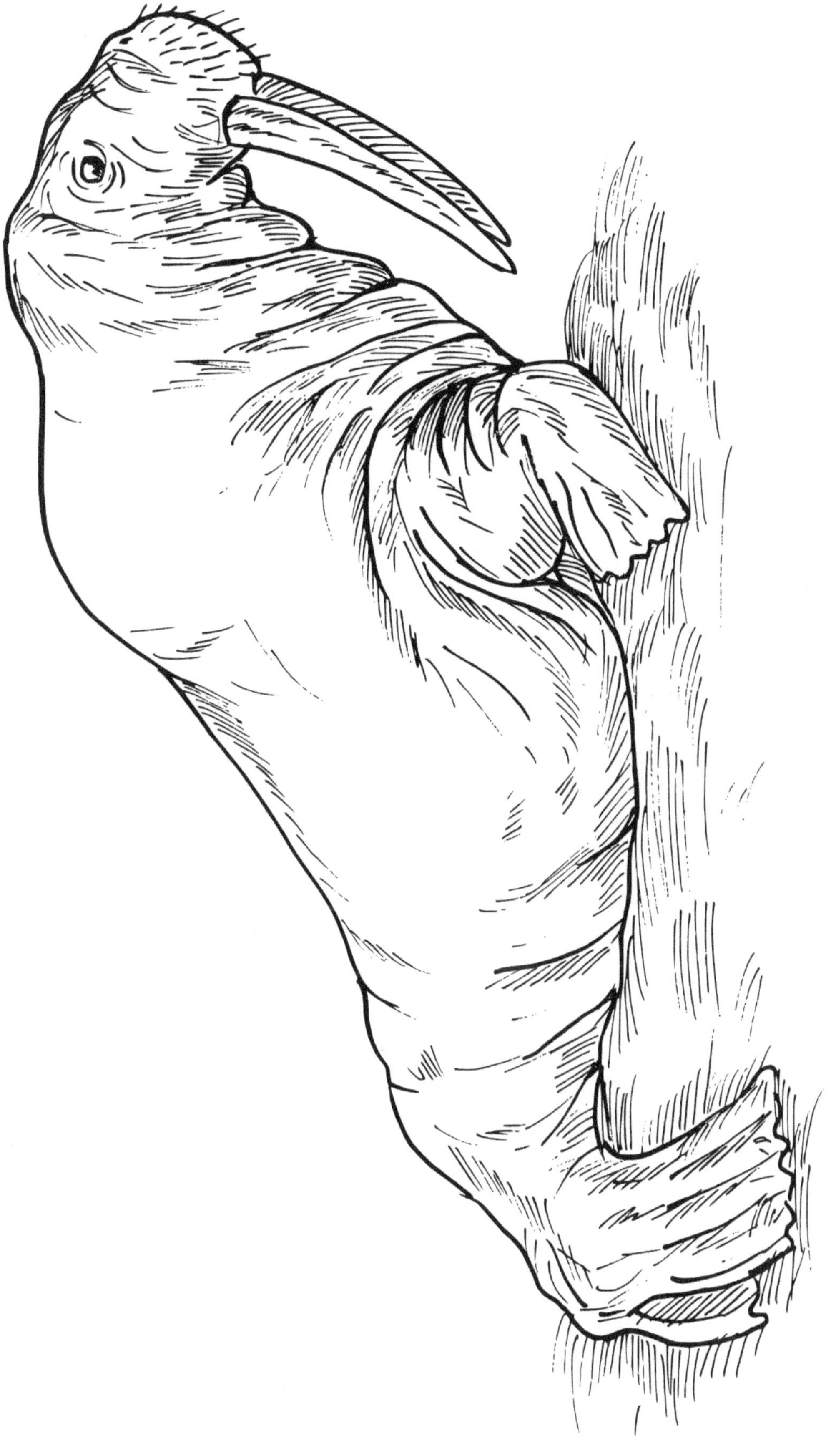

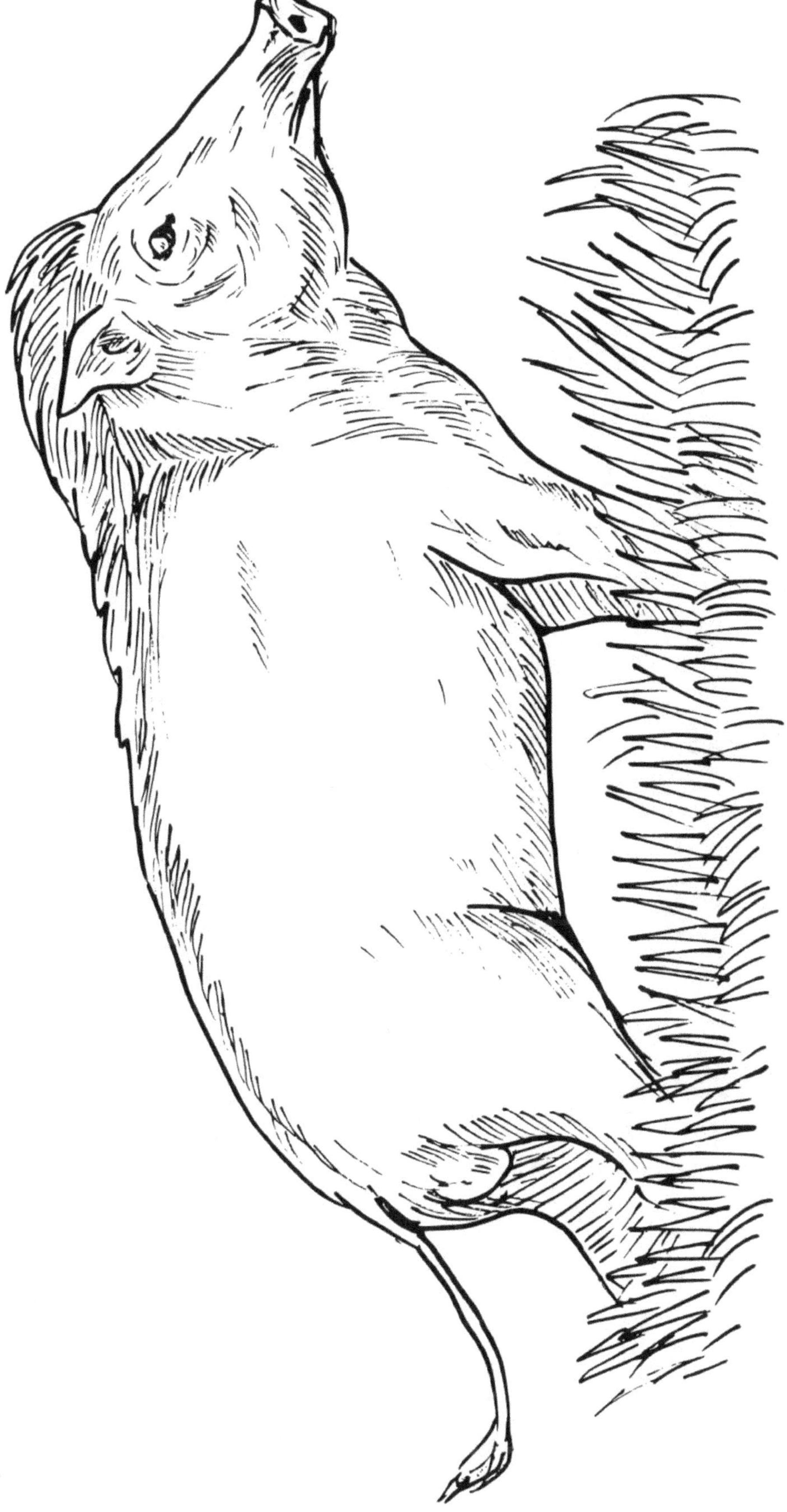

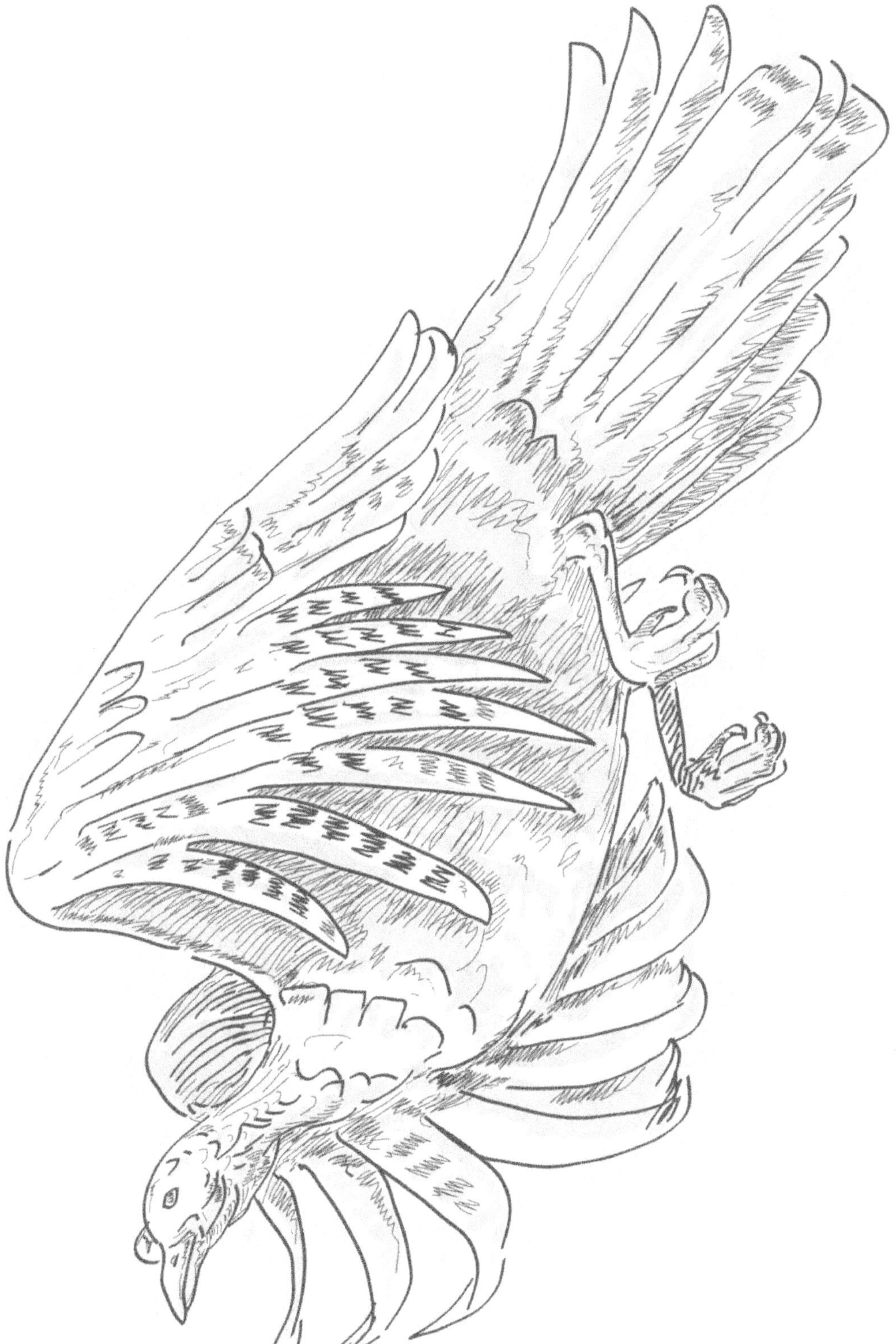

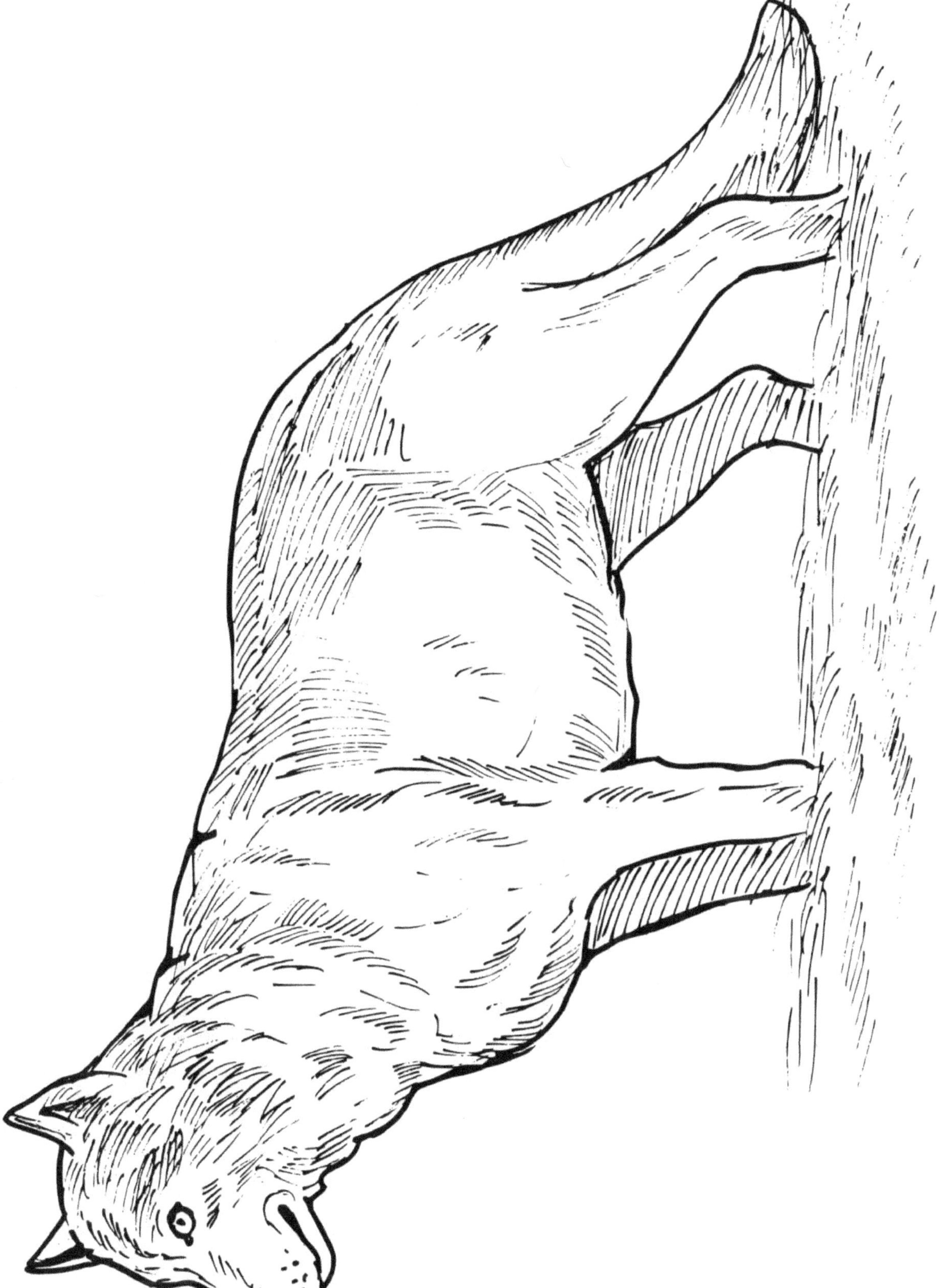

ZEBRA

www.ingramcontent.com/pod-product-compliance
Lightning Source LLC
Chambersburg PA
CBHW081118280526
45787CB00007B/2884
9781535158077